A Worm Bin

BY KIM THOMPSON

A Little Honey Book

Crabtree Publishing
crabtreebooks.com

Tips for Teachers and Caregivers

This book supports early readers as they decode words to learn facts and gain knowledge about the world.

Before reading, make sure students understand the sound-spelling correspondences shown below as well as the high-frequency words shown on the next page. Introduce the vocabulary words.

During reading, provide feedback and encouragement as students sound out decodable words by blending individual sounds.

After reading, talk about and write about the topic. Share the information on page 16 to help students learn more.

Letters and Sounds

New:

Sound	Spelling
/b/	b
/r/	r

Review:

Sound	Spelling
short a	a
/k/	c
/d/	d
/f/	f
/g/	g
/h/	h
short i	i

Sound	Spelling
/m/	m
/n/	n
short o	o
/p/	p
/s/	s
/t/	t

Decodable Words

bad, big, bin, bits, dig, gob, in, is, it, not, rid, rim, rip, rots

High-Frequency Words

New: eat, for, get, go, good, of

Review: a, helps, old, out, the, to, water, we

Vocabulary Words

food

plants

poop

worms

We rip bits.

Bits go in a bin to the rim.

Worms go in the bin.

A big gob of worms!

We water the bin.

The bin helps get rid of old **food**.

The worms eat the bits of food.

The worms **poop**.

Worm poop rots.

We dig it out.

Worm poop is not bad.

It is good food for **plants**!

plants

Build Background Knowledge

Vermicomposting, or worm farming, uses worms to make nutrient-rich compost for your garden. Red wigglers are the best worms to use. Placed in a bin filled with moist bedding, they will eat vegetable scraps and produce castings, or worm poop. These castings make some of the best compost for plants. Instead of sending food scraps to a landfill in a trash bag, you can use them to enrich the soil in your own yard.

Written by: Kim Thompson
Designed by: Rhea Magaro
Series Development: James Earley
Educational Consultant: Marie Lemke, M.Ed.

Photographs: All images from Shutterstock

Crabtree Publishing

crabtreebooks.com   800-387-7650
Copyright © 2025 Crabtree Publishing
All rights reserved. No part of this publication may be reproduced, stored in a retrieval system or be transmitted in any form or by any means, electronic, mechanical, photocopying, recording, or otherwise, without the prior written permission of Crabtree Publishing.

Printed in China/012024/FE20231222

Published in Canada
Crabtree Publishing
616 Welland Ave.
St. Catharines, Ontario
L2M 5V6

Published in the United States
Crabtree Publishing
347 Fifth Ave
Suite 1402-145
New York, NY 10016

Library and Archives Canada Cataloguing in Publication
Available at Library and Archives Canada

Library of Congress Cataloging-in-Publication Data
Available at the Library of Congress

Hardcover: 978-1-0398-4431-5
Paperback: 978-1-0398-4512-1
Ebook (pdf): 978-1-0398-4589-3
Epub: 978-1-0398-4659-3
Read-Along: 978-1-0398-4729-3
Audio: 978-1-0398-4799-6